DEL AMITRI
OTHER SUCKERS
PARADE

POLYGRAM MUSIC PUBLISHING LIMITED

EXCLUSIVE DISTRIBUTORS: MUSIC SALES LIMITED 8/9 FRITH STREET, LONDON W1V 5TZ, ENGLAND. MUSIC SALES PTY LIMITED 120 ROTHSCHILD AVENUE, ROSEBERY, NSW 2018, AUSTRALIA.

ORDER NO. AM950378 ISBN 0-7119-7021-1 THIS BOOK © COPYRIGHT 1997 BY POLYGRAM MUSIC PUBLISHING LIMITED VISIT THE INTERNET MUSIC SHOP AT http://www.musicsales.co.uk

MUSIC ARRANGED BY ROGER DAY. MUSIC PROCESSED BY PAUL EWERS MUSIC DESIGN.

YOUR GUARANTEE OF QUALITY: AS PUBLISHERS, WE STRIVE TO PRODUCE EVERY BOOK TO THE HIGHEST COMMERCIAL STANDARDS. THE MUSIC HAS BEEN FRESHLY ENGRAVED AND, WHILST ENDEAVOURING TO RETAIN THE ORIGINAL RUNNING ORDER OF THE RECORDED ALBUM, THE BOOK HAS BEEN CAREFULLY DESIGNED TO MINIMISE AWKWARD PAGE TURNS AND TO MAKE PLAYING FROM IT A REAL PLEASURE. PARTICULAR CARE HAS BEEN GIVEN TO SPECIFYING ACID-FREE, NEUTRAL-SIZED PAPER MADE FROM PULPS WHICH HAVE NOT BEEN ELEMENTAL CHLORINE BLEACHED. THIS PULP IS FROM FARMED SUSTAINABLE FORESTS AND WAS PRODUCEDWITH SPECIAL REGARD FOR THE ENVIRONMENT. THROUGHOUT, THE PRINTING AND BINDING HAVE BEEN PLANNED TO ENSURE A STURDY, ATTRACTIVE PUBLICATION WHICH SHOULD GIVE YEARS OF ENJOYMENT. IF YOUR COPY FAILS TO MEET OUR HIGH STANDARDS, PLEASE INFORM US AND WE WILL GLADLY REPLACE IT.

MUSIC SALES' COMPLETE CATALOGUE DESCRIBES THOUSANDS OF TITLES AND IS AVAILABLE IN FULL COLOUR SECTIONS BY SUBJECT, DIRECT FROM MUSIC SALES LIMITED. PLEASE STATE YOUR AREAS OF INTEREST AND SEND A CHEQUE / POSTAL ORDER FOR £1.50 FOR POSTAGE TO: MUSIC SALES LIMITED, NEWMARKET ROAD, BURY ST. EDMUNDS, SUFFOLK IP33 3YB.

PRINTED IN THE UNITED KINGDOM BY HALSTAN & CO LIMITED, AMERSHAM, BUCKS.

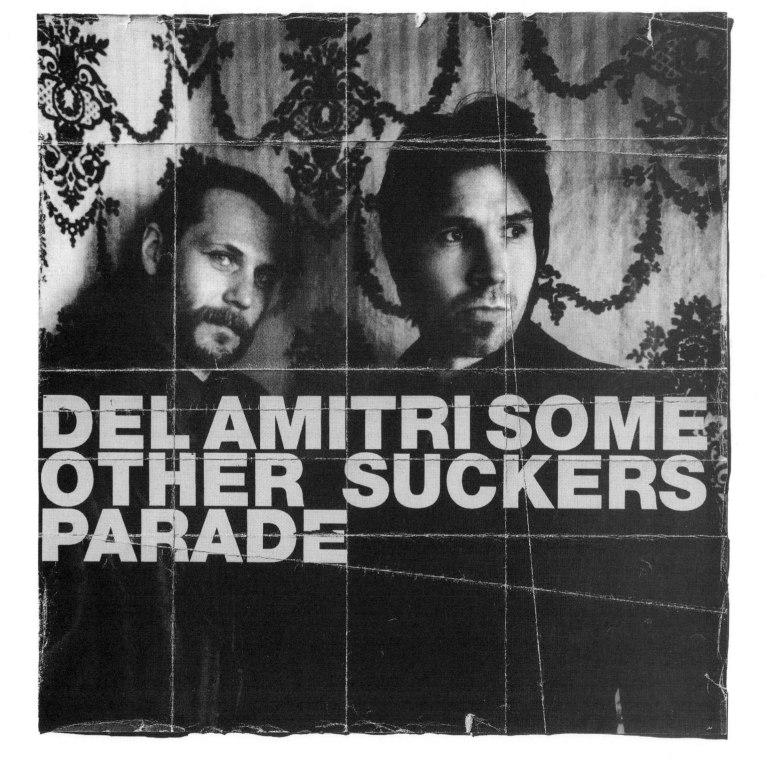

NO FAMILY MAN. 44.
CRUEL LIGHT OF DAY. 48.
FUNNY WAY TO WIN. 37.
THROUGH ALL THAT
NOTHING. 52. LIFE IS
FULL. 57. LUCKY GUY. 62.
MAKE IT ALWAYS BE
TOO LATE. 67.

NOT WHERE IT'S AT

WORDS & MUSIC BY JUSTIN CURRIE

and some girls they are

ea - sy   to be your - self ___ with,   but the

one girl that I want ___   ain't ea - sy ___ to ___ please

__ with what I've got. ___

Yeah,— I'm— not— where— it's— at.—

Verse 2:
With some girls it don't matter where you're aiming
With some girls it don't matter how you act
And some girls they don't care what car you came in
But the one girl that I want
She wants that one bit of geography I lack.

Verse 3:
And some girls they will worry about reactions
And some girls they don't give a damn for that
And somehow I ain't ever in on the action
'Cause the one girl that I want
She wants that one little quality I lack.

SOME OTHER SUCKER'S PARADE

WORDS & MUSIC BY JUSTIN CURRIE & JOHN McLOUGHLIN

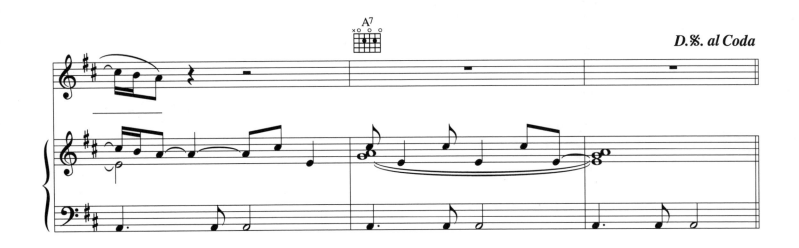

⊕ *Coda*

Verse 2:
I've had my share of heartaches,
Let downs and tricks,
But the every day blues is the one thing I can fix.
I've heard those holy brethren
Muttering my name,
But it ain't no sin to drink when you're suffering.

Patience they say, is a saintly virtue,
But hell, why should I wait
Till the clouds go rain on some other sucker's parade.

D.%.
8 bars instrumental

So if the road of sin is the one I'm taking
I ain't gonna stray
Till the clouds go rain on some other sucker's parade.

WON'T MAKE IT BETTER

WORDS & MUSIC BY JUSTIN CURRIE & IAIN HARVIE

want to throw a - way the old you, but the old you's old e - nough to know it won't make it bet - ter, it won't make it bet - ter. 2. Sick of be - ing a los-

So you—

-ter, it won't make it bet-

-ter, it won't make it bet-ter,

it won't make it bet-ter, it won't make it

WHAT I THINK SHE SEES

WORDS & MUSIC BY JUSTIN CURRIE

♩=104

1. I've been in this place many times be - fore,
(Verses 2 & 3 see block lyric)

with my ba - by's things a - mong my shoes and strings and

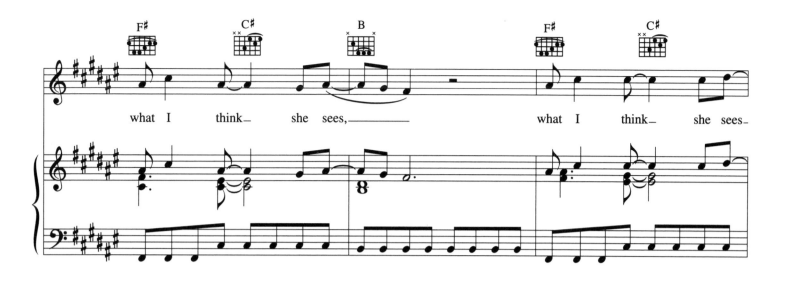

what I   think___   she sees,_____   what I   think___   she sees_

___   ain't   me   at   all.___

Verse 2:
Baby likes to sleep on floorboards bare
And just to keep the peace well I join her there
But she might say to me
"A better man I can't recall"
But what I think she sees ain't me at all.

Verse 3:
Baby claims I kiss like I really care
Well I guess I'd say I don't, but the truth ain't fair
And sometimes she looks at me and says
"Babe my heart just stalled"
But what I think she sees
What I think she sees
What I think she sees ain't me at all.

MEDICINE

WORDS & MUSIC BY JUSTIN CURRIE

1. Well you can find an-oth-er coun-try if you want,—
(Verses 2, 3 & 4 see block lyric)

some-where you can hide your-self a-way,——— find your-self an-oth-er

set of holes to haunt— get your-self an-oth-er debt that you— can't pay.——

D.%. al Coda

4. Yeah you can on-ly try to

Coda

that makes the pain.

Verse 2:
Yeah you can try to run for cover everywhere
Add another letter to your name
Burn everything you ever used to wear
Get yourself another lover that looks the same.

Verse 3:
You can always make another move again
Another set of keys, a different town
And you can try to lose yourself in them
Till the truth it catches up and cuts you down.

Verse 4:
Yeah you can only try to fool yourself so long
With any kind of measure you can find
'Cause every phoney pleasure you've been on
Has lifted off and left the pain behind.

HIGH TIMES

WORDS & MUSIC BY JUSTIN CURRIE & IAIN HARVIE

she's got a right___ to be la___zy

flat out of rea-sons to breathe.___ And it's cold___ ba - by,___ yes it's cold,

___ ___ but ev - 'ry-thing is re - la - tive.___ Can't you see we're liv - ing in

high times,___ dig the new do -

Verse 2:
Little Snow White, she was hungry
Told her, go out and graft for it
At the end of the rainbow, she was mind blown
To be staring at a crock of shit.

And it's hard baby, yes it's hard
But with a little intuition
　　　you can shift position in the...

High times,
Touch the magic stone
Living through high times
Pick up that spiritual phone.

Verse 3:
Frittering packs of refuseniks
Too drunk to master any contempt
Ten ways to relax on a cruise ship
One way to cover the rent.

I've whored myself around enough to know baby
You don't come with the customers and smile
　　　when you spoken to in...

High times,
Catch the cosmic vibe
Living through high times
Hey, has Ginger Baker died?

MOTHER NATURE'S WRITING

WORDS & MUSIC BY JUSTIN CURRIE & IAIN HARVIE

1. Op - en up your eyes, ev - 'ry - thing is
(Verses 2, 3 & 4 see block lyric)

cry - ing out, this could be your time.

35

Verse 2:
She fell out of the sky
Must every star been working on
Heavenly designs.

Verse 3:
So button up your lip
You don't get many chances in
The time between the tides.

Verse 4:
The weather's rolling in
In a minute flat you'll be soaking wet
So kiss her while it's dry.

FUNNY WAY TO WIN

WORDS & MUSIC BY JUSTIN CURRIE & IAIN HARVIE

win.

So if there's an - oth - er need that I can ___ still serve ___

low on self es - teem but I'm high ___ on ___ nerve. ___ *Solos*

win.

Yeah that's a fun - ny way to win.

Yeah that's a fun - ny way to win.

NO FAMILY MAN

WORDS & MUSIC BY JUSTIN CURRIE

and you talk like a ba - by___ when your boy___ is

cry - ing, you made some - thing___ to love,

but I love what___ I am, no fa - mi - ly man.

2. So don't tell me___ you've

Verse 2:
So don't tell me you've got
Something better than me,
Don't say
That it's a great mystery.
It's just making love
What you want it to be.
That's why I am
No family man.

Verse 3:
Have you got something to prove
With your own little you,
Have I wasted my time
Cut through the family line,
In the race to life
I am an also-ran,
But I've run enough
To know I'm no family man.

CRUEL LIGHT OF DAY

WORDS & MUSIC BY JUSTIN CURRIE

3. Said

No

I ain't some ac - ces - so - ry—— she can slip off from her back— and just fold a - way,—

I don't need no one un - dress-ing me,— when I

wake up   in the same___ suit ev - 'ry - day.___

4. Said

Coda

No I don't   see it   in the   cruel   light of day.___

Verse 2:
Tell him he's done me a kindness
She was gonna leave anyway.
But love is such sweet blindness
When I see it in the cruel light of day.

Verse 3:
So pour me another cup of coffee
I ain't never seen the city look so grey
And those pretty little diamonds in the darkness
Ain't no jewels in the cruel light of day.

Verse 4:
Said someone's opening up for business
The shutters roll so familiarly
And out of the darkness comes release sing the witless
I don't see it in the cruel light of day.

THROUGH ALL THAT NOTHING

WORDS & MUSIC BY JUSTIN CURRIE & IAIN HARVIE

out of bed ___ in sur - prise.

In the ___ bright ___ morn - ing sun,

___ in the howl - ing wind, ___ in the shirt you sleep ___

___ in you're the one. 'Cause ___ it's

54

So it's true now,—— I——— can see——

all—— that no - thing—— that I knew——

——— was so—— some - thing—— like—— you'd—— come——

to me.———————

Verse 2:
The hands of fate
Couldn't have done it all
As if the rain ever cared where it falls
And there were times
When I know that
I just fell in love to give myself an alibi.

'Cause it's you I was waiting for
Every day and every night
Through all that nothing,
Through all that nothing.

LIFE IS FULL

WORDS & MUSIC BY Justin Currie

1. Peo - ple say you are a stand up guy,
(Verses 2 & 3 see block lyric)

you'd nev - er hurt no one and you'd nev - er try, and you

Verse 2:

Friends say you are a careful man
You always favour reason where you can
And you laugh and you cry
And you do all the things that anybody does
To show they are alive.

Verse 3:

People say you are a patient guy
You never rush something if it ain't right
And you laugh and you cry
And you do all the things that anybody does
To show they are alive.

LUCKY GUY

WORDS & MUSIC BY JUSTIN CURRIE & IAIN HARVIE

1. Ba - by hold — it, just let me try —
(Verse 2 see block lyric)

D.%. al Coda

Un - luck - y for some.

Repeat to fade

So luck - y ba - by.

Verse 2:
Baby I like it
It feels alright
Now that I see it through his cheating eyes,
I can't stop smiling.

How could I not be satisfied
So glad I ain't the one on the losing side.

D.%.
So I don't know where tonight
Love will lead me, but that's alright 'cause…

66

MAKE IT ALWAYS BE TOO LATE

WORDS & MUSIC BY JUSTIN CURRIE

1. What I want is ev-'ry-thing to clear.

(Verses 2 & 3 see block lyric)

So let the clocks be wrong, let the

So get late.

Verse 2:
'Cause what I want
Gets clouded by the sun
I can't see beyond
The petty things that living here brings everyone.

Verse 3:
'Cause what I want
Is right before my eyes
Set me up a drink
Pull the shutters down on all those prying satellites.